Running Aground

poems by

Elizabeth Joy Levinson

Finishing Line Press
Georgetown, Kentucky

Running Aground

ACKNOWLEDGMENTS

Apple Valley Review: "Homecoming"
Entropy: "Broken Water;" "Close;" and "When we were children, we were
mermaids"
Hobble Creek Review: "Recovering"
LandLocked: "Insufficient Funds"
Slipstream: "Exterminator"
Whale Road Review: "Florida Girl"

Publisher: Leah Maines
Editor: Christen Kincaid
Cover Art: Amanda Levinson
Author Photo: Jason Terrill
Cover Design: Elizabeth Maines McCleavy

Printed in the USA on acid-free paper.
Order online: www.finishinglinepress.com
also available on amazon.com

Author inquiries and mail orders:
Finishing Line Press
P. O. Box 1626
Georgetown, Kentucky 40324
U. S. A.

Table of Contents

for Michael and Cheryl,
whom I would choose again and again,
even though I didn't

Insufficient Funds

I am sorry I have existed, taken up space, opened my mouth and spoken or opened my mouth and did not speak. I stepped on a butterfly. I stepped on a crack. I stepped on concrete. Someone put concrete down for me to step on. I bought a dress. I did not buy a dress. I did not make myself beautiful, with painted lips and laughter. I was unkind. I was a different kind. I was a stereotype. I was the kind of girl who could not hold her horses.

I begged for the horses. I left the horses in the pasture. I left the horses out in the rain. The horses were on an island and the shoreline was eroding.

I abandoned the land. I did not have enough boards. I did not bring enough nails. I left as my toes were getting wet.

I was a good daughter. I sent a check.

The portrait of an addict as the elements

The fire you set inside yourself,
you know you lit the match even

water is heavy, the way your body
is heavy, the way you just noticed
you can't lift your own arm, like
every muscle has water bags strapped
or every appendage is being pulled
by a rip current in an opposite direction.

The room is pulled until it is hard to recognize.
Walls buckle but the flame does not.
You cave into the earth, you wish
you could have caved
into your mother's arms but she was not
that kind of mother. She was as easy to hold onto
as air, maybe that's why you started smoking
at twelve, you wanted a mother you could hold onto,
you could hold air in your lungs, you could hold the smoke
until it became a part of you.

When we were children, we were mermaids.

In water, in snow, when we are tuck tired in a wet sleep,
in a saturated dream, these are my hands in the sink,
these are my feet in the ocean,
and I'm holding my breath,
with my lungs somewhere in between.
We were always under or in or maybe
just off to the side, intracoastal
water, wander, wanderer.
We needed only carry our bodies
through the waves,
enough that we were too tired to notice
all we left behind.
We were always swimming,
even when we were not, when we
were wrapped in towels,
laid out on the shore,
legs bound in cotton curls of terry cloth
too tired to remember
where we had come from and
where we were going to.

Florida Girl

Florida girl is eating a stalk of celery with peanut butter and sand. She is trying not to choke. Florida girl knows about flannel moth caterpillars and puss caterpillars, how soft they look and how dangerous their fur. Florida girl is always chasing her baby brother, who can hit a lizard with a rock dead, despite that he is only three and doesn't ever want to wear clothes. Florida girl has an illegal pet tortoise. Her father almost hit it and said it would have died. She feeds it lettuce and lawn. Florida girl has rich friends, which she shouldn't. They take her to amusement parks. Once, she lost twenty dollars at Busch Gardens and cried over it for weeks. Her Florida sister works at a bakery for less than minimum wage because she is less than minimum age and she brings home day old bread sometimes. Florida girl drinks orange juice from the oranges in the yard. Florida girl has sand in her food because she is always at the beach. When Florida girl's scholarship dries up, she transfers to public school, where she is bullied mercilessly. One day, in geography, she stands on a desk and yells "Leave me the fuck alone." And miraculously, they do, everyone, the teachers don't even call her parents. Florida girl wishes she had yelled anything else instead. Florida girl never has the right words. The Gulf of Mexico swallowed them all.

Things no one told my parents and, also, why I got a D in geography

Try understanding geography when
the map is always changing, when
the world is holding
a magnet to your compass,
the pin marking "you are here"
isn't a pin at all, but the silver ball
of a pinhead rolling around
to the sound of the ocean.

They were listening for the sound
of the ocean and maybe
they were listening
in all of the wrong places.
A tin can can sound
like a conch if you want it to.
The conch is only an illusion anyway,
who is to say where
that magic comes from.

For me, it came from the car stereo,
ballads on breathing and rain
in smooth synth and well enunciated lyrics.
How easy to pretend
you were a song story
when there was no place
your story belonged.

No one told them how hard it is
to anchor anything to the ocean.
How easy to drag
until you don't recognize
the shoreline you end up on.

At the Party

The Gondolier in
brown polyester pants
and red and white bateau neck
moves across the floor
like the tracks
in his arms
are grooves
in the wood
he can slide through
jump over
pivot and return
and do it
all over
again.

Every poem is about my father

Is what I tell people at parties, when they ask.
It is as true to say as it is true to say that every poem is an apology
or that every poem is an origin story. They may be one in the same.
I am always using my father to excuse my own misbehaviors.
When I was a child, I kept things, a wild menagerie
of secret insects, salamanders, snakes, usually
they died before they could be released.
I was building a curio of guilt, so I would have walls
that lasted around me where the walls were so quickly
coming down, being rebuilt, changing shape.
We were ephemera in the world,
we moved so quickly,
I'm not sure if I was there or just a ghost,
a scale of a girl, now a fishwife,
I don't yet know how to live with people,
I think I have it down
and then I open my mouth.

The Fire-Eater

He learned the trick in the army,
where he spent two years
inspecting food and getting high-
mealworms swimming in sacks of flour,
they must have plagued
the dreams in his veins, but
this is the nature of his narrative,
no matter how many times I hear it,
it is difficult to knit these bones together,
to understand how he progresses
from one event to another,
are these the joints that haven't set right,
hands always cupped but empty?

Either way, there was always a motorcycle,
Japanese of some make
and he was in the German countryside
stoned out of his mind,
and he came upon a circus.

I hope he doesn't mind it,
but I imagine him surrounded
by sequined girls and clowns
and fire eaters
thrusting burning batons towards him
before extinguishing the flames in their own throats,
it was a trick he learned to perform,
one of many he used to keep us enthralled,
before we understood anything at all,
how basic a thing it is,
to deprive a fire of oxygen.

Leaving

In the back of the old station wagon,
one sister on each side of me
like strangers, they are to me
negotiating the room between
our legs stretched over suitcases,
our laps an array of toys, of books.

Amanda twists her lips, her eyes squint
for the benefit of other kids in other cars.

Rebecca sleeps, tired from so much riding
her legs are too long, they are growing everyday now
they are twisted at odd angles,
her lungs heave loudly, sucking down
the re-circulated air.

There is no novelty here.
We've done this before.
Because we are gypsies
or poor, or because my parents
see promise in everything—

my gaze sweeps over my sisters
but holds on the landscape.
On the edge of the street
the budding leaves
look different
everywhere we go.

Exterminator

In Florida,
you tried everything
but you couldn't kill the insects
faster than they could hatch
so you taught me about them instead.
I learned to identify
orb weavers
mole crickets.
I kept a close watch
when they came out
just before dawn
to drink
from condensation
on blades
of tangled crabgrass.

Those mornings,
I wove my toes
into the stubborn plant's runners,
grainy soil stuck to my skin.
as the sun heated up,
the smell of rotting oranges
so high in the gnarled tree,
we could never pick them all.

You moved on,
sold solar panels,
adjustable beds,
insurance. Roaches multiplied,
we could not keep up.

In the evenings, we rinsed in the ocean,
we were never clean,
never refreshed,
but we were tired,
we slumbered dreamlessly.

Eventually, all that wasn't living
sank into brown shag
behind white stucco walls
built on crawfish, cockroaches.
They scurried between our feet,
watching, as we fled, left our things:
plastic Legos, silverware, socks.
Hidden from us, much later
we realized they were gone.

We left those things and
the salt-heavy air
the way the moisture collected on skin,
with sweat and hot dog grease.

It was better that way,
to leave,
the ocean always burned
my thighs chafed inside
and eyes red

as the ink on the eviction slip
and the tongues of the lizards flicking
as they ran across the door.

Homecoming

After eight months at sea
he still hasn't found his land legs,
my father walks in feebly.

We must seem as mermaids,
more bitter than benevolent,
dragging him from his ship.

At dinner, he repeats himself,
a joke that no one hears,
every time, he gets a little louder.

When his feet take a more steady gait
I notice the way my mother's dress
catches the light when he spins her.
Does he see cheap lamé
or scales against her skin?

He has gone completely gray.
His hair is cut too short.
When he stands next to her,
he looks older than my mother.

Later, while dancing he says,
"You will only be able to have
half the things you want in life."

He dips me, and for a moment,
I find myself pulling him down again
without even trying.

Hurricane

Gloria came in '85,
had us huddled
in the coatroom,
under a cloak
of wool and down,
the acridity of once living things
reduced to useful artifacts.

Everyone knows to
avoid anything glass, but
you took me out the French doors
in the eye of the storm,
the air charged and warm
it wasn't raining but
my skin felt damp
and the sky, the purple-yellow
of a new bruise.

I was seven.
Was this the first time I felt brave?
or the first time I felt defiant?
And I wonder
which of the two led you
to bring me through
holding tight to my hand,
as the wind picked up,
and took our laughter
from our lungs.

My Father's Hands

I damn my fingers, child-like digits
dry, a woman's skin older than mine.
They bleed easily, they split in the cold,
around the knuckles and the nails
where they are creased the most.

So soft
even knitting can sting,
even cashmere yarns
can chafe and leave me raw.

Your hands more calloused,
thick pads of dead skin built up on each tip
and you, always so impatient with me.

I could never hold the line,
never pull quickly enough.
It burned too much.

You sat me down
when I was five,
made me watch as you brought
right thumb to right forefinger
and stitched the two together, the black thread
a dead worm under your waxy flesh.
The snap when you pulled the thread
pulled tight my chest.

When you tied off, you looked at me,
your hand held together like a shadow rabbit,
you danced it around in front of me,
showing off your embroidery.

You laughed until I laughed, until you knew
that I knew you were okay.
I wanted hands like that.

My nephew leans his head into my hand.
His skin, like peach, like lamb's ear, the downy leaves
of mullein pink, but different, a slight nuance
you would not feel.
He says, "Papa sewed his fingers together,"
and he's agitated by the simple trick, concerned.

I stroke his forehead, ruffle his hair, explain
about calluses and how they form and why.
Today—my hands as I wanted them to be—
today, my hands are mine.

Close

As children, we would find them
deflated sacks flat against the land.
Kicking up the Atlantic
brought moon jellies to the shore,
their tentacles already shriveling
rendered impotent
by the air and the sand.

Once, I drifted in those waters
over a grouper lounging
at the bottom of the ocean
his mouth gaped wide.
I still recall the taste
as I tried to get closer
and the water filled the snorkel
that was keeping me in air
I surfaced, choking and sputtering
and by the time I recovered, he was gone.

There is no way of knowing
how these memories may
weigh me down more
than any other.

Another time, I was bewildered.
Ten feet below me a green turtle swam,
his flippers waving, beckoning me closer,
but the current was strong and
threatened to rake me
over fire corals,
and I came so close
but there was a jelly,
it almost brushed my cheek
I lost sight of the turtle
as I righted myself in the water.
It was nothing.
Another day.

Broken Water

In the V-berth, I was re-birthed.
Every morning, I rose before my shipmates and
went above to watch the sun
appear in the horizon.

Throughout the day, I baked.
Sometimes small pustules formed on my skin,
pearly and taut,
tiny and smart, they broke away
when I brushed my hands over my arms
and felt that small relief of the water,
leaking out and spreading over me
before evaporating. We are all part sea.

Overcoming the tiller, learning the way the lady moved,
I was new. Each day, each different passing landscape,
I was new. Every time we came into port,
I liked to sound out my new language,
One hand on the life line, the other throwing out a rope,
and when I stepped off the boat,
I shook the hands that caught and tied me off safely.
Each time, they were new hands.

And in each port,
I tried new paces,
new swings, new words,
I was moving.

At night, I showered on the deck,
sun heated water in a bag
hanging on the mast.

My shipmates were two strangers
or, one was my father
the other, a lover.
It didn't really matter.
There was no way of knowing
that could have overcome:
the changes in the water
were predictable.

I was not.

Some Men Bring Flowers

The house I bought was in disrepair
the yard overgrown
nightshade and thistle almost as tall as I.
A marijuana plant,
lone, therefore useless
was hidden in the weeds.
When my father came
to help with the plumbing and electric
I pointed it out and he quickly cut a leaf from the plant
for my mother who, inspired by some TV show
has been thinking of starting
a medicinal marijuana farm.

My father wants to sail to Cuba,
he's making plans with a few other boaters
who have done it before.
He says, tell your mother nothing.

Months later, I visit them,
my father hasn't left yet,
my mother has hung
the nine-pointed leaf on the fridge
in a flat wax bag
its fingers dried and curled.
I imagine that if I took it out
it would crumble in my hand.

Emergency Procedures

He's got a hand on the tiller,
and his sights on the sea
and the strength in his arms
carries through the lines, up the mast
moving us forward
while my own legs
lock around the lazarette
and my thighs clench tighter every time
we keel, 15, 20 degrees, and when
I can almost reach the water,

he asks, *what would you do now
if something happened to me?*

and I do not cry while he explains
how to sail into the wind
how to bring the ship to a dead stop at sea
so I can take the main down before
seeing to the patient, before the *mayday...*

mayday, mayday

A loggerhead comes up for air, it is right beneath the surface,
and I point it out—this is my protest.

In time, barnacles will build whole worlds
on the bottom of a boat abandoned at the township dock,
the captain landlocked, me and my sisters will argue
on the best way to care for him
and he will be so diminished. And we will be so wrong.

And I do not want to know this, that it will not be so easy
as finding the wind and sailing into it,
watching the canvas go slack
with little luffing,
with little fight.

Recovering

Some days he travels for hours
at best, makes seven knots
and sees no one.
The waters are charted,
but these edges of the Intracoastal,
too soft and too green.
Like the history of his veins,
they are murky.

In the waters
no one asks him to speak
no one tells him to stop talking
the dolphins don't care what he does,
they flank the sides of the boat,
they may stay with him for a while,
or not.

It's okay, alone
running aground,
the keel buried in silt.
He waits,
as the tide rises
he floats away.

When he passes through more solid territory
buildings take footing and floodlights
falsely pull creatures from the sea
shorelines take shape.

Forty years ago
there were nights on the beach
when he slept soundless as the sand
that stuck to his cheeks
but even here,
in slow currents
it continues to compel him.
Standing with the tiller between his legs
he gently shifts away.
Where he sees no one
neither is he seen.

Everything

The white fingers
of the sycamores
reach out
against the cerulean sky,
the moon white and translucent,

Am I white and reaching and translucent?

I am white and reaching and translucent.
I am a killing frost at dawn
or an ice storm

I am trying
to hold everything
at once.

Elizabeth Joy Levinson was born in Chicago and has spent her entire adult life in the second city, but spent much of her childhood in transit, spending time in New York, Florida, and Nevada. She teaches at Wendell Phillips High School, on the city's south side and coaches her school's Louder Than A Bomb poetry team. She has an MFA in Poetry from Pacific University and an MAT in Biology from Miami University. She lives with her husband, artist and photographer, Jason Terrill, and their dog and two cats.

Her work has appeared in several journals, including *Grey Sparrow, Up the Staircase, Apple Valley Review, Hawk and Whippoorwill, LandLocked, Whale Road Review,* and *Slipstream.* Her first chapbook, *As Wild Animals,* is available through Dancing Girl Press.

CPSIA information can be obtained
at www.ICGtesting.com
Printed in the USA
JSHW031237231020
8964JS00002B/140

9 781646 622795